W9-DEA-482

Reading Mastery
Signature Edition

Storybook I

Siegfried Engelmann
Elaine C. Bruner

McGraw Hill SRA

Columbus, OH

SRAonline.com

 SRA

Printed in the United States of America.

Send all inquiries to this address:
SRA/McGraw-Hill
4400 Easton Commons
Columbus, OH 43219

ISBN: 978-0-07-612458-9
MHID: 0-07-612458-4

12 13 14 15 DOW 13 12

The **McGraw·Hill** Companies

Contents

the cow on the rōad

lots of men went down the rōad in a littl_e car.

a cow was sitting on the rōad. sō the men ran to the cow. "wē will lift this cow," they said.

but the men did not lift the cow. "this cow is sō fat wē can not lift it."

the cow said, "I am not sō fat. I can lift mē." then the cow got in the car.

the men said, "now wē can not get in the car." sō the men sat on the rōad and the cow went hōm_e in the car.

the end

pāint that nōse

a fat dog met a littlе dog.
the fat dog had a red nōse. the
littlе dog had a red nōse.

the fat dog said, "I havе a
red nōse."

the littlе dog said, "I wish I
did not havе a red nōse."

the fat dog got a can of
pāint. hē said, "pāint that nōse."

sō the littlе dog did pāint her
nōse. shē said, "now this nōse is
not red." shē kissеd the fat dog
on the ēar. now the fat dog has
pāint on his ēar.

the end

rēad the Ītems

1. when the tēacher says "gō,"
   stand up.

2. when the tēacher says "gō,"
   clap.

---

whȳ	the
that	shē
them	of
therₑ	fōr
wherₑ	dōn't
when	didn't
then	hērₑ
ātₑ	her

rēad the Ītems

1. wнen the tēₐcher says "now," clap.

2. wнen the tēₐcher says "now," stand up.

---

did	thōse	arₑ
clap	thēsₑ	farm
do	therₑ	yard
of	then	her
fōr	whȳ	hērₑ
dōn't	wнen	at
didn't	werₑ	ātₑ
very	wнerₑ	hē
every	her	shē
ēven	hērₑ	thē

rēₐd the Ītem

when the tēₐcher says "do it,"
stand up.

the talkiñg cat

the girl was gōiñg fōr a
walk. shē met a fat cat. "can
cats talk?" the girl said.

the cat said, "I can talk, but
I do not talk to girls. I talk to
dogs."

the girl did not lĪkₑ that cat.
"I do not lĪkₑ cats that will not
talk to mē."

the cat said, "I will not talk
to girls."

the girl said, "I do not lIke
that cat. and I do not give fish
cāke to cats I do not lIke."

the cat said, "I lIke fish
cāke, sō I will talk to this girl."

sō the girl and the cat āte
the fish cāke.

the end

rēₐd the Ītem

when the tēₐcher says "do it,"
clap.

diggiñg in the yard

a littlₑ man had a big dog.
the big dog livₑd in the yard. hē
dug a hōlₑ in the yard. the littlₑ
man got mad. hē said, "dogs can
not dig in this yard. I will gō
fōr a cop."

but the dog dug and dug.

the man got a cop. the man
said, "that dog dug a big hōlₑ in
the yard."

the cop said, "dogs can not dig in this yard."

the dog said, "I will stop. can I bē a cop dog?"

the cop said, "yes. I nēēd a cop dog."

the end

rēₐd the Ītem

when the tēₐcher says "gō," clap.

will the ōld car start?

a man had an ōld car. the ōld car did not start. sō hē went down the rōₐd. soon hē cāmₑ to a big man.

hē said, "can you start an ōld car?"

the big man said, "yes, I can but I will not. I am sittiñg. and I never start cars when I am sittiñg."

the man said, "you can sit in the car if you can start it."

sō the big man got in the car and māde the car start. hē said, "I līke this ōld car. sō I will kēēp sitting in it." and hē did.

the end

rēad the Ītems

1. when the tēacher says "now,"
   hōld up your hand.

2. when the tēacher says "gō,"
   hōld up your hands.

---

start	hēre	them
barn	there	then
shark	of	when
can't	fōr	where
can	end	whȳ
this	live	how
that	līked	didn't
the	lived	dōn't
hē	shē	did
her	they	do

rē_ad the Ītems

1. when the tē_acher says "do it,"
   hōld up your hands.
2. when the tē_acher stands up,
   clap.

---

hard	wher_e	fōr
farm	when	of
ar_e	then	hē
do	they	the
did	shē	that
dōn't	liv_ed	this
didn't	lĪk_ed	ther_e
how	liv_e	hēr_e
whȳ	end	her

the dog and the bath

wē had a big dog. her nāme was sal. this dog līked to run and plāy. this dog did not līke to take a bath.

wē said, "come in, sal. it is tīme to tāke a bath." wē ran after her.

wē said, "sal, if you come back and tāke a bath, you can have some cōrn." but shē did not līke cōrn.

wē said, "if you come back and tāke a bath, you can have some mēat." but shē did not līke mēat.

wē said, "if you come back

and tāke a bath, you can rēad a book."

the big dog cāme back and took a bath. whȳ did sal tāke a bath? shē līked to rēad books.

this is the end.

arf the shark

arf was a barking shark. arf was a little shark, but shē had a big bark that māde the other fish swim awāy.

a shark swam up to arf and said, "you are a shark. let's plāy."

arf was happy. "arf, arf," shē said. and the other shark swam far, far awāy. arf was not happy now.

another shark swam up to arf. "you are a shark," hē said. "let's plāy."

arf was happy. "arf, arf," shē said. and the other shark

swam far, far awāy. arf was
not happy now.

then a big, big fish that līked
to ēat sharks swam up to the
other sharks.

"help, help," they yelled.

but the big fish was
swimming after them very fast.

stop

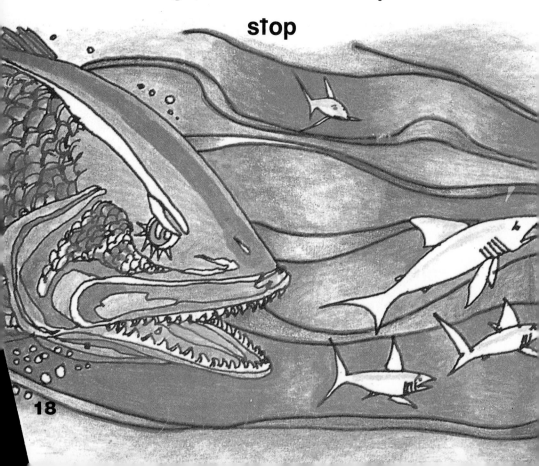

18

arf can help

arf was a barking shark. the other sharks did not līke her big bark. when arf went "arf, arf," the other sharks swam awāy.

but now arf had to help the other sharks. a big fish that līked to ēat sharks was gōing after the other sharks. arf swam up to the big fish and said, "arf, arf." the big fish swam far, far awāy.

the other sharks līked arf now.

"wē līke arf now," they said.

and now arf plāys with the other sharks. and if a big fish

that līkₑs to ēₐt sharks swims
up to them, arf says "arf, arf."
and the big fish swims far, far
awāy.

the end

rēad the Ītems

1. when the tēacher stands up, clap.

2. when the tēacher claps, hōld up your hand.

---

lĪked	barkin͡g	when
swim	that	there
fōr	hēre	other
get	shē	funny
got	they	hōrse
end	where	cāme
and	how	give
at	whȳ	trȳin͡g
āte	dōn't	rĪdin͡g
ēat	didn't	hard

rēₐd the Ītem

wh̟en the tēₐcher says "stand up,"
sāy "gō."

the cow boy and the cow

a cow boy was sad. hē did
not haveₑ a hōrseₑ. the other cow
boys said, "hō, hō, that funny
cow boy has nō hōrseₑ."

a cow cāmeₑ up to the cow
boy. the cow said, "if you areₑ a
cow boy, you nēēd a cow. I am
a cow."

the cow boy said, "do not bē
funny. cow boys do not rIdeₑ on
cows."

the cow said, "but I can run
as fast as a hōrse. and I can
jump better than a hōrse."

the cow boy said, "I will
give you a trȳ. but I will fēēl
very funny rīdiṅg on a cow." sō
the cow boy got on the cow.

then the other cow boys
cāme up the rōad. "hō, hō," they
said. "look at that funny cow
boy. hē is trȳiṅg to rīde a cow."

stop

rēad the Ītem

when the tēacher says "now,"

pick up your book.

the cow boys haVe
a Jumpiñg mēēt

the cow boy got on a cow.

the other cow boys said, "hō, hō.

that is funny."

the cow boy got mad. hē

said, "this cow can gō as fast as

a hōrSe. and Shē can Jump better

than a hōrSe."

the other cow boys said, "nō cow can jump better than mȳ hōrse." sō the cow boys rōde to a crēēk.

the cow boy on the cow said, "let's sēē if a hōrse can jump this crēēk."

"I will trȳ," a cow boy said. his hōrse went up to the crēēk. but then his hōrse stopped. and the cow boy fell in the crēēk.

the cow boy on the cow said, "hō, hō. that hōrse didn't ēven trȳ to jump the crēēk."

the next cow boy said, "mȳ hōrse will trȳ. and mȳ hōrse will flȳ ōver that strēam.

hē will not ēven touch the strēₐm."

mōrₑ to come

rēad the Ītem

when the tēacher says "stand up,"
hōld up your hand.

the cow boys trȳ

some cow boys māde fun of
a cow boy that rōde a cow. they
said, "nō cow can jump better
than a hōrse." sō they rōde to a
crēēk to sēē if a cow could
jump better than a hōrse.

a cow boy fell in the crēēk.
now the next cow boy was gōiñg
to māke his hōrse jump ōver the
crēēk. his hōrse went very fast.
the hōrse cāme to the bank of

the crēēk. then the hōrs_e jumpₑd. did hē gō to the other sīd_e? nō, hē went splash in the crēēk. the cow boy was mad.

the next cow boy said, "I will trȳ to jump ōver that crēēk. and I hav_e the best hōrs_e in the land."

but that cow boy's hōrs_e went splash and the cow boy fell in the crēēk. the cow boys said, "wē did not jump that crēēk, but that fat cow can not jump as far as a hōrs_e."

"let's sēē," said the cow boy with the cow. the cow started to run faster and faster and faster. the cow ran up to the bank of the crēēk. and then the cow jumped.

stop

r̄ead the Ītem

when the tēacher says "clap,"
touch your f̄ēēt.

the happy Jumpin͡g cow

the cow boy on the cow was
tr̄yin͡g to Jump ōver the crēēk.
the cow ran to the bank and
Jumpₑd with a big Jump.

the cow Jumpₑd ōver the
crēēk. the cow did not touch the
strēam. the other cow boys
lookₑd at the cow. they said,
"we arₑ wet and cōld." but the
cow boy on the cow was not
wet. and hē was not cōld.

hē gāve the cow a kiss. and
hē said, "now I fēel līke a rēal
cow boy. thōse other cow boys
can have a hōrse. I will stāy with
this jumping cow." and hē did.

hē rōde the cow. hē jumped
ōver rocks with the cow. hē had
that cow fōr yēars and yēars.
and nō other cow boy ever
māde fun of his cow after the
cow jumped ōver the crēēk.

the end

rēₐd the Ītems

1. when the tēₐcher stands up, sāy "gō."

2. when the tēₐcher says "do it," hōld up your hands.

3. when the tēₐcher says "stand up," hōld up your hand.

of	better	circle
fōr	faster	farmer
and	you	start
how	didn't	where
other	crȳiñg	when
strēam	flȳiñg	them
this	after	then
hēre	thiñgs	what
there	gōiñg	that
whȳ	touch	thōse

rēad the Ītems

1. when the tēacher says "do it," touch your fēēt.

2. when the tēacher stands up, hōld up your hands.

jill and her sister

this is the stōry of a girl nāmed jill and her sister. jill trīed to do thinḡs, but her sister did not trȳ.

jill said, "I can not rīde a bīke, but I will trȳ."

what did jill sāy?

her sister said, "I can not rīde, but I do not līke to trȳ."

soon jill rōde a bīke, but her sister did not. her sister started to crȳ. jill said, "if you trȳ, you will not have to crȳ."

then jill said, "I can not jump rōpe, but I will trȳ."

what did jill sāy?

her sister said, "I can not jump rōpe, but I do not līke to trȳ."

soon jill jumped rōpe, but her sister did not. her sister said, "I can not jump rōpe, sō I will crȳ."

jill said, "if you trȳ, you will not have to crȳ."

more to come

rēad thè Ītems

1. when the tēacher claps, touch your head.

2. when the tēacher says "clap," touch your fēēt.

jill trĪed and trĪed

did jill trȳ to do thiñgs?

did her sister trȳ to do thiñgs?

what did jill do when shē trĪed?

jill said, "Ī can not rēad a book, but Ī will trȳ."

what did jill sāy?

her sister said, "I can not
rēₐd a book, but I will not trȳ."

what did her sister sāy?

sō Jill trĪₑd to rēₐd and her
sister did not trȳ.

now Jill is good at rēₐdiñg.
but her sister can not rēₐd
books. her sister can not rĪdₑ a
bĪkₑ. her sister can not Jump
rōpₑ. and her sister can not
rēₐd books. but her sister can
do some thiñg better than Jill.
her sister can rēₐlly crȳ.

this is the end.

rēₐd the Ītems

1. when the tēₐcher stands up,
   pick up your book.
2. when the tēₐcher stands up,
   touch your heₐd.

jon bākes a fish cāke

a boy nāmₑd jon was gōin͡g
to bāke the best cāke hē ever
māde. hē said, "I will trȳ to
bāke a fish cāke."

hē askₑd his brother, "will
you help mē bāke a fish cāke?"

what did hē ask?

his brother said, "ick. a fish
cāke? I hāte fish cāke." hē ran

into the yard to plāy.

Jon askₑd his sister, "will you help mē bākₑ a fish cākₑ?"

what did Jon ask?

his sister said, "ick. a fish cākₑ? I rēally do not līkₑ fish cākₑ." then his sister ran into the yard to plāy.

Jon ēven askₑd his mother, "will you help mē bākₑ a fish cākₑ?"

what did Jon ask?

but his mother said, "ick. fish cākₑ? ick."

sō Jon mādₑ the fish cākₑ him self.

mōrₑ to come

rēad the Ītems

1. when the tēacher says "clap," touch your nōse.

2. when the tēacher says "gō," sāy "fĪve."

jon hātes fish cāke

what kĪnd of cāke did jon bāke?

did his sister help him?

did his mother help him?

jon māde the fish cāke bȳ him self.

when hē sat down to ēat the cāke, his brother cāme in. his

brother asked, "can I trȳ some of that fish cāke?"

what did hē ask?

Jon said, "you didn't help mē bāke the cāke, sō you dōn't have to help mē ēat it."

Jon's mother and Jon's sister cāme in. they asked, "can wē trȳ some of that fish cāke?"

what did they ask?

Jon said, "you did not help mē bāke the cāke. sō you dōn't have to help mē ēat the cāke."

sō Jon āte the fish cāke bȳ him self. then hē got very sick. now hē hātes fish cāke. if you ask him to help you bāke fish

cāke, hē will sāy, "ick. I hāte
fish cāke."

what will hē sāy?

the end

rēₐd the Ītems

1. when the tēₐcher stands up, sāy "you arₑ standiñg up."
2. when the tēₐcher claps, pick up your book.

spot

this is a stōry of a dog nāmₑd spot. spot did not hēₐr well. the other dāy shē went to a stōrₑ to get some bōnₑs. the man in the stōrₑ said, "it is a fīnₑ dāy."

"what did you sāy?" spot askₑd.

tell spot what the man said.

the man got some bōnes fōr spot. hē said, "pāy mē a dīme fōr thēse bōnes."

spot askₑd, "what did you sāy?"

tell spot what the man said.

spot did not hēaʳ the man and the man was gettiñg mad at spot. the man said, "givₑ mē a dīme fōr thēse bōnes."

spot askₑd, "what did you sāy?"

tell spot what the man said.

spot said, "it is tīmₑ fōr mē to lēaᵥe. sō I will pāy you a dīme fōr the bōnes and I will gō hōmₑ."

sō spot gāve the man a dīme.
then shē took the bōnes hōme
and had a fīne mēal of bōnes.
the end

rēad the Ītem

when the tēacher hōlds up a
hand, touch the flōōr.

spot and the cop

this is another stōry of spot
the dog.

did spot hēar well?

one dāy spot went fōr a
walk to the other sĪde of town.
when shē got there, shē said, "I
can not fĪnd mȳ wāy back
hōme."

what did shē sāy?

shē walked and walked. but
shē did not fĪnd the strēēt

that led to her hōme. shē
started to crȳ.

then a big cop cāme up to
her. spot said, "I trīed and
trīed, but I can not fīnd mȳ
wāy back hōme."

the cop said, "wherₑ do you
livₑ?"

spot said, "what did you
sāy?" tell spot what the cop said.

spot still did not hēar what
the cop said. sō the cop got a
pad and māde a nōte fōr spot.
the nōte said, "wherₑ do you
livₑ?"

spot read the nōte and said,
"I livₑ on broom strēēt."

the cop said, "I will tāke you
to broom strēēt." and hē did.
spot kissed the cop and said,
"some dāy I will pāy you back.
you are a good cop."

the end

rēad the Ītems

1. when the tēacher stands up, pick up your book.
2. when the tēacher says "touch your fēēt," touch your fēēt.

the boy askₑd whȳ

a boy nāmₑd don lĪkₑd to ask whȳ. his mother tōld him to stāy in the yard. hē askₑd, "whȳ?" sō shē tōld him whȳ. shē said, "wē will ēₐt soon." what did shē sāy?

don dug a big hōlₑ in the yard. his brother said, "you must not dig hōlₑs in the yard."

don asked, "whȳ?" sō his brother tōld him. his brother said, "hōles māke the yard look bad." what did his brother sāy?

don got a can of whīte pāint. "I will pāint mȳ bīke whīte," hē said. sō hē got the pāint brush and started to pāint his bīke.

his sister asked, "what are you doing?"

don answered, "pāinting mȳ bīke whīte."

what did the boy sāy?

mōre to come

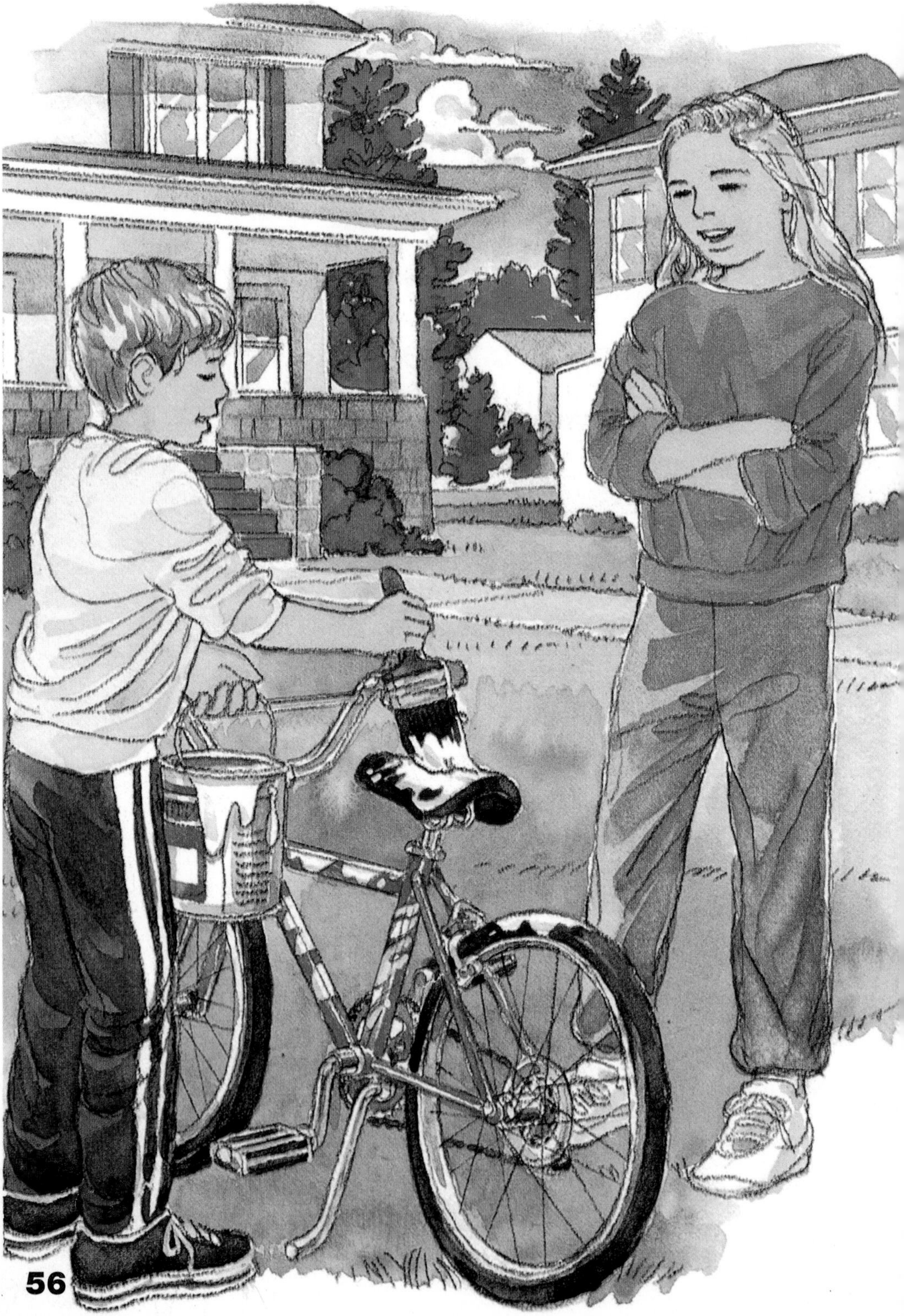

rēad the Ītem

when the tēₐcher stands up, sāy "stand up."

don pāinted and pāinted

what did don lĪkₑ to ask?

what did hē do in the yard?

what did hē start to pāint?

who askₑd him what hē was doiñg with his bĪkₑ?

his sister said, "that looks lĪkₑ fun." sō shē got a pāint brush and started to pāint don's bĪkₑ.

don and his sister pāinted the bĪkₑ. then don said, "whȳ

dōn't wē pāint the sīde walk?"
what did hē sāy?

sō they pāinted the sīde walk.
what did they do?

then they pāinted the steps
to don's hōme.

then they pāinted a rock.

and then they pāinted ēach
other.

then don's mom went into the
yard. shē was mad. shē said, "you
pāinted the bīke, the steps, the
rock, and ēach other."

what did shē sāy?

what do you think shē did to
don and his sister?

the end

rēad the Ītems

1. when the tēacher says "fēēt," touch your fēēt.

2. when the tēacher says "stand up," hōld up your hands.

spot helps the cop

spot was walkiñg nēar a stōre. robbers cāme from the stōre with bags of monēy. a big cop ran to stop the robbers. hē yelled, "drop that monēy." but the robbers did not drop the monēy. the robbers had a big hōrn and they started to blōw it. "toot, toot," the hōrn went.

"I can not stand the 'toot, toot' of the hōrn," the cop said. "it mākₑs mȳ ēₐrs sōrₑ."

the cop held his hands ōver his ēₐrs. then the robbers ran bȳ him. the hōrn was still gōin͡g "toot, toot."

the hōrn did not mākₑ spot's ēₐrs sōrₑ. spot did not ēven hēₐr the hōrn. sō spot ran up to the robbers. spot bit them on the legs. they droppₑd the big hōrn. they droppₑd the monēy. then the cop stoppₑd them.

hē said to spot, "you helpₑd stop the robbers." what did hē sāy?

the big cop was very happy.
the end

rēad the Ītem

when the tēₐcher picks up a book,
sāy "hands."

flȳiñg is fun

a littlₑ bird had six sisters.
his sisters said, "come and flȳ
with us." but the littlₑ bird did
not flȳ. sō hē started to crȳ.

his sisters said, "wē did not
sāy to crȳ with us. wē said to
flȳ with us. stop crȳiñg and start
flȳiñg."

but the littlₑ bird did not
stop crȳiñg.

his sisters said, "whȳ arₑ

you crȳiñg?" what did they sāy?

the littlᴇ bird said, "I am crȳiñg bēcause I cannot flȳ."

whȳ was hē crȳiñg?

his sisters said, "wē will tēₐch you to flȳ if you stop crȳiñg."

sō the littlᴇ bird stoppᴇd crȳiñg. then his sisters grabbᴇd him and took him up, up, up into the skȳ.

then they said, "you arᴇ a bird, sō you can flȳ."

they let gō of him. hē yellᴇd, "I can flȳ."

now when the sisters sāy "let's flȳ," the littlᴇ bird ᴊumps

up and down. hē says, "yes, flȳiñg
is mōr_e fun than crȳiñg."

then the littl_e bird and his
sisters flȳ and flȳ.

what do they do?

the end

rēₐd the Ītems

1. when the tēₐcher says "go," sāy "fĪvₑ."

2. when the tēₐcher stands up, sāy "now."

the farmer and his buttons

a farmer lĪkₑd buttons. he had red buttons and gōld buttons. he had lots of big buttons and lots of littlₑ buttons. he had buttons on his hat and buttons on his socks. he ēven had buttons on some of his buttons. but he had his best buttons on his pants. he had ten big buttons on his pants.

one dāy a man cāme to the farm. the man said, "I have come to buȳ buttons." he looked at the buttons on the farmer's pants. "I will buȳ that big red button," he said.

so the farmer took off the big red button and sōld it. now he had nīne big buttons on his pants.

then the man said, "now I will buȳ that big gōld button."

so the farmer took off the gōld button and sōld it. now the farmer did not have nīne buttons on his pants. do you think the man will bu**ȳ** m**ōr**e buttons from the farmer?

m**ōr**e to come

rēₐd the Ītem

wнen the tēₐcнer says "go,"
toucн your heₐd.

the farmer sōld нis buttons

wнat did the farmer līkₑ?

wнerₑ did нe нavₑ нis best
buttons?

wнat did the man want to buȳ
from the farmer?

the man kept buȳiñg buttons
and the farmer kept selliñg them.
the man said, "now you нavₑ fīvₑ
buttons. I want to buȳ that pink
button." so the farmer took off
нis pink button and sōld it to
the man.

then the man wanted to buȳ
the farmer's yellōw button. so
the farmer sōld the yellōw
button to the man.

the man said, "you still haveₑ
thrēē buttons. I will buȳ them."

so the farmer took off the
thrēē buttons. but when his
pants had no mōreₑ buttons, his
pants fell down. what did they
do?

the farmer said, "mȳ pants
fell down bēcause I sōld the
buttons that held up mȳ pants."
what did he sāy?

so now the farmer has
monēy, but he has no buttons to

kēēp his pants up. how will he
kēēp his pants up?

this is the end.

rēₐd the Ītem

when the tēₐcher says "clap,"
touch your fēēt.

spot tākₑs a trip

one dāy spot said, "I want to
go on a trip in mȳ car." so she
did.

she got in her car and went
down the rōₐd. soon she stopped.
she askₑd a man, "whₑre can I
get gas?"

the man said, "on best
strēēt."

spot said, "whₑre did you
sāy?"

tell spot what the man said.

so spot went to best str$\overline{ee}$t and got gas. then she went down the r$\overline{o}$ad some m$\overline{o}$re. soon she stopped. she asked a l$\overline{a}$dy, "where is the town of dim?"

the l$\overline{a}$dy said, "dim is f$\overline{I}$ve m$\overline{I}$les down the r$\overline{o}$ad."

spot asked, "where did you s$\overline{a}$y?"

tell spot what the l$\overline{a}$dy said.

and spot went to the town of dim. then spot stopped and asked a man, "where is a st$\overline{o}$re that sells b$\overline{o}$nes?"

the man said, "go down to m$\overline{a}$in str$\overline{ee}$t."

"wher_e did you sāy?" spot
ask_ed.

tell spot what the man said.

so spot went to the stōr_e
and got a bag of bōn_es. she
had a good trip.

the end

r̄ead the Ītems

1. when the t̄eacher says "what," touch your n̄ose.

2. when the t̄eacher stands up, s̄ay "sit down."

3. when the t̄eacher says "do it," h̄old up your hands.

park	hēre	calling
are	whȳ	hall
shark	līkes	of
barn	wanted	for
farm	stopped	thōse
what	very	thēse
want	ēven	that
were	all	them
where	fall	they
there	call	when

rēₐd the Ītem

wℎen the tēₐcℎer says "now,"
clap.

the dog lĪkes to talk, talk, talk

a tall man ℎad a dog that
lĪked to talk and lĪked to rēₐd.

one dāy the dog was rēₐdiñg
a book. the tall man was in the
ℎall. ℎe callₑd the dog. ℎe yellₑd,
"dog, come ℎēre and plāy ball
with me."

the dog yellₑd back at the
man, "I ℎēₐr you call, call, call,
but I dōn't lĪke to plāy ball,
ball, ball."

the man was getting mad. he
yelled, "dog, stop rēading that
book and start plāying ball."

she yelled, "I will not go
into the hall, hall, hall, and I will
not plāy ball, ball, ball."

the man was very mad now.
he cāme into the room and got
his cōat. he said, "well, I am
gōing for a walk. do you want to
come with me?"

the dog said, "I will not do
that, that, that, when I can sit
hēre and get fat, fat, fat."

so the tall man left and the
dog went back to her book.
she said, "I hāte to walk, walk,

walk, but I līke to talk, talk, talk."

the end

rēad the Ītem

when the tēₐcher says "do it,"
hōld up your hand.

the small bug went to
livₑ in a ball

therₑ was a small bug that
did not havₑ a hōmₑ. he went to
livₑ in a tall trēē. but a big
ēₐglₑ said, "this is mȳ tall trēē.
go look for another hōmₑ."

then the bug livₑd in a hōlₑ.
but a mōlₑ said, "that's mȳ
hōlₑ. go look for another hōmₑ."

then the small bug livₑd on a
farm in a box of salt. but a cow

said, "that's mȳ salt. go awāy or
I'll ēat you up when I lick mȳ
salt."

then the small bug livₑd in a
stall on the farm. but a hōrsₑ
said, "what arₑ you doīng in mȳ
stall? go fīnd another hōmₑ."

at last the bug went to a
hōmₑ nēₐr the farm. he spotted a
ball on the flōōr. the ball had a
small hōlₑ in it. the bug said, "at
last I sēē a hōmₑ for me." he
went into the ball and sat down.
he said, "I hōpₑ that I can stāy
in this ball. I līkₑ it hērₑ."

mōrₑ to come

rēad the Ītem

when the tēacher says "go," sāy
"stand up."

the bug in the ball mēēts a girl

a small bug had a hōme in a
ball. he said, "I hōpe I can stāy
in this ball. I lĪke it hēre."

he went to slēēp in the ball.
he was having a good drēam. he
was drēaming of a fĪne party.
then he sat up. the ball was
rōlling. "what is gōing on?" he
called.

he looked from the little
hōle in the ball and saw a tall

girl. she was rōlliñg the ball on the flo͞or.

"what arₑ you doiñg?" he asked. "this is mȳ hōmₑ. stop rōlliñg it on the flo͞or."

the girl pickₑd up the ball and lookₑd at the small bug. then she droppₑd the ball. "ōh," she crīₑd, "therₑ is a bug in mȳ ball. I hātₑ bugs."

the ball hit the flo͞or. it went up. then it went down. then it went up. the bug was gettiñg sick.

"stop that," he callₑd. "I dōn't līkₑ a hōmₑ that gōₑs up and down."

the tall girl bent down and
looked at the bug. she said,
"this is mȳ ball. so go awāy."
the small bug looked up at
the girl and started to crȳ.
mōre to come

rēₐd the Ītem

wnen the tēₐcher stands up, sāy
"you arₑ standiñg up."

the bug wants to stāy
in the ba!!

a small bug wanted to livₑ
insĪdₑ a ball. but a tall girl tōld
him that he must lēₐvₑ the ball
and fĪnd another hōmₑ. the small
bug started to crȳ. he said,
"whₑrₑ will I go? I cannot livₑ in
a tall trēē. I cannot livₑ in a box
of salt. I cannot livₑ in a hōrsₑ
stall. and now I cannot stāy in
this ball."

"stop crȳiñg," the girl said. "I can't stand to sēē small bugs crȳ."

the bug said, "if you let me stāy in this ball, I will plāy with you."

"no," the girl said. "I dōn't plāy with bugs. I hāte bugs."

the bug said, "I can siñg for you. I will ēven let you come to the party that I am gōiñg to have in mȳ ball."

she said, "dōn't be silly. I can't fit in that ball. look at how tall I am."

the bug called, "let me stāy."

the girl sat down on the

flōōr and looked at the small
bug. "I must think," she said.
what was she gōīng to think
ōver?

mōre to come

rēₐd the Ītem

when the tēₐcher says "go,"
touch your arm.

the tall girl bets her
brother

a tall girl wanted the bug to
lēₐve the ball and fĪnd another
hōmeₒ the bug crĪₑd and tōld
her all the thin͡gs he would do if
she let him stāy in the ball. he
said that he would sin͡g for her.
he said that he would let her
come to his party in the ball.

the girl was sittin͡g on the
flō͞or thinkin͡g of the bug.

then her brother cāme into
the room. he said, "what are you
doing?"

she said, "go awāy. I am
thinking."

he said, "do you think that
the ball will start rōlling if you
look at it very hard?" her
brother did not sēē the bug
insīde the ball.

the girl said, "if I want this
ball to start rōlling, it will
start rōlling. and I dōn't ēven
have to touch it."

her brother said, "I'll bet
you can't māke that ball rōll
if you dōn't touch it."

"how much will you bet?" the girl asked. she looked at the bug and smīled.

her brother said, "I will bet you one football and ten toy cars."

the girl said, "I will tāke that bet."

mōre to come

rēₐd the Ītem

when the tēₐcher says "stop,"
touch the flōōr.

the tall girl wins the bet

the tall girl mād e a bet with
her brother. she bet him that she
could māk e the ball start rōlliñg.
she said, "I dōn't ēven hav e to
touch it."

her brother did not sēē the
bug in the ball. so he bet one
football and ten toy cars.

the girl lookₑd at the ball and
said, "start rōlliñg, ball." the

bug started runniñg insĪde the
ball. he ran and ran. he ran so
fast that the ball started to rōll.

the girl's brother lookₑd at
the ball. he said, "wow. that ball
is rōlliñg and you arₑ not ēven
touchiñg it."

the girl said, "Ī tōld you Ī
could māke the ball rōll."

so the girl got one football
and ten toy cars.

then she said to the small
bug, "you helpₑd me win the bet,
so Ī will let you stāy in mȳ ball.
this ball is your hōme now."

the bug was so happy that
he ran from the ball and kissₑd

the girl on her hand. "thank you, thank you," he said.

and nēₐr the end of the wēēk, he had a fīnₑ party insīdₑ his ball. every bug on the strēēt cāmₑ to the party, and they all said that it was the very best party they ever had.

the end

rēₐd the Ītem

when the tēₐcher says "go," hōld up your hands.

the elephant gets glasses

a small elephant was not happy bēcause he alwāys fell down.

one dāy he went for a walk. he could not sēē the tall trēē. so he hit his heₐd on the tall trēē and fell down.

he said, "whȳ do I alwāys fall down? I wish I would not fall. I hāte to fall."

he walked some mōre. he could not sēē a big red ball. so he fell ōver the big red ball.

the small elephant said, "whȳ do I alwāys fall down? I hāte to fall."

he walked some mōre. but he could not sēē all the boys and girls ēating hot dogs. he could not sēē the pīle of hot dogs. so he fell into the hot dogs.

the boys and girls got mad. "how could you fall into thōse hot dogs?" they said. "do you nēēd glasses?"

the elephant said, "I have never sēēn glasses."

so a tall girl took her glasses
and gāve them to the elephant.
the elephant trīed on the glasses.

"mȳ, mȳ," the elephant said.
"now I can sēē all kīnds of
thiñgs. I can sēē tall trēēs, balls,
and hot dogs."

now the small elephant is
happy bēcause he has glasses.
and he never falls down.

this is the end.

the dog loves to rēₐd, rēₐd, rēₐd

a dog that could talk livₑd with a tall man. the dog took a book from the tābl. the dog said, "this book is what I nēēd, nēēd, nēēd. I love to rēₐd, rēₐd, rēₐd."

the tall man cāmₑ in and said, "I look, look, look, but I cannot sēē mȳ book, book, book."

then the man said, "mȳ book was on the tābl."

the dog said, "the book was on the tābl, but I took it from the tābl."

the tall man yellₑd at the dog.

he said, "you must not tāke mȳ book from the tābl₍ₑ₎."

she said, "do you want to plāy ball, ball, ball in the hall, hall, hall?"

"yes, yes," the man said.

the dog kickₑd the ball far, far, far down the hall. when the man ran after the ball, the dog took the book and hid it.

then she said, "let the man look, look, look. he will never fīnd his book, book, book."

the end

walter wanted to plāy football

walter loved to plāy football. but walter could not plāy well. he was small. and he did not run well. when he trīed to run with the ball, he fell down. "dōn't fall down," the other boys yelled. but walter kept falling and falling.

when walter ran to get a pass, he dropped the football. "dōn't drop the ball," the other boys yelled. but walter kept dropping balls.

dāy after dāy walter trīed to plāy football, but dāy after dāy he fell down and dropped the ball.

then one dāy, the other boys said, "walter, you can't plāy ball with us any mōre. you are too small.

you alwāys fall. and you alwāys
drop the football."

walter went hōme and sat in his
yard. he was mad. he said to himself,
"I am small and I cannot run well."
walter wanted to crȳ, but he
didn't crȳ. he sat in his yard
and felt very sad. when his mom
called him for dinner, he said, "I
dōn't want to ēat. I must sit hēre
and think."

more to come

walter gōes to the big gāme

walter was sad bēcause the other boys would not let him plāy football with them. walter was still sad on the dāy of the big football gāme. the boys that lived nēar walter were plāyiñg boys from the other sīde of town.

walter went down to the lot where the boys plāy football. he said, "I can't plāy in the gāme bēcause I alwāys fall. but I will look at the big gāme."

there were lots of boys and girls at the football lot. some of them were chēēriñg for the boys that lived nēar walter. other boys and girls were chēēriñg for the tēam that cāme from the other sīde of town.

the gāme started. therе was a tall boy on the other tēam. that tall boy got the football and ran all the wāy down the lot. he scōred. the boys and girls from the other sIdе of town chēēred.

walter's tēam got the ball. but they could not go far. they went fIvе yards.

when the other tēam got the ball, the tall boy kickеd the ball. it went to the end of the lot for another scōrе. walter said to himself, "that other tēam is gōing to win. I wish I could help mȳ tēam."

mōrе to come

walter gōes in the gāme

walter was lookиng at the big football gāme. walter's tēam was not doiиg well. the other tēam had 2 scōres. but walter's tēam did not have any scōres. as the gāme went on, walter's tēam started to plāy well. walter's tēam stopped the tall boy when he got the ball. then walter's tēam scōred. walter chēēred. he yelled, "get that ball and scōre some mōre."

but then the best plāyer on walter's tēam cut his arm. he left the gāme. walter said to himself, "now we cannot win the gāme. the best plāyer is not plāyиng."

how could walter's tēam win if the best plāyer was not plāyиng?

then all the boys on walter's tēam started to call. "walter, walter," they called. "come hēre."

walter ran to his tēam. one of the boys said, "walter, we nēēd one mōre plāyer. so we called you. trȳ to plāy well. we nēēd 2 scōres to win this gāme."

mōre to come

walter's tēam must kick

walter's tēam called him to plāy
in the big gāme.

one of the boys on walter's
tēam said, "we cannot run with the
ball, bēcause the best runner is
not in the gāme. so let's trȳ to
scōre bȳ kickiñg the ball."

"yes, yes," the other boys said.

then the boys looked at ēach
other. "one of us must kick the ball."

all the other boys said, "not me. I
can't kick the ball that far."

but walter didn't sāy "no." he
said, "I will trȳ. I think I could kick
the ball that far."

one of the boys said, "I will
hōld the ball for him."

so walter got ready to kick the
ball. some boys and girls called
from the sīde of the lot, "dōn't let
walter do that. he can't plāy football.
he will fall down."

but walter said to himself, "I will
not fall. I will kick that ball." and
walter felt that he would kick the
ball.

mōre to come

walter kicks the ball

walter was ready to kick the ball. the boys and girls on the sīde of the lot were sāyiñg, "dōn't let walter kick."

but walter did kick. another boy held the ball. a tall boy from the other tēam almōst got to the ball, but walter kicked the ball Just in tIme. the ball went lIke a shot. it went past the end of the lot. it went ōver a tall wall that was next to the lot. it almōst hit a car that was on the strēēt.

the boys on walter's tēam looked at walter. the boys on the other tēam looked at walter. one boy from the other tēam said, "that ball went all the wāy ōver the wall. I did not think that a small boy could kick a ball so far."

the boys and girls on the sīde of the lot chēēred. "that's the wāy to kick, walter," they callₑd.

now walter's tēam nēēded one mōrₑ scōrₑ to win the gāmₑ.

mōrₑ to come

walter's tēam wins

the other tēam did not scōre. so walter's tēam got the ball.

one boy on walter's tēam said, "we must go all the wāy down the lot to scōre. but we dōn't have tĪme and we can't kick the ball that far."

walter said, "I think I can kick the ball all the wāy." so the boys on walter's tēam got ready.

the ball went into plāy. a boy from walter's tēam held the ball, and walter kicked it. it went all the wāy to the end of the lot. it almōst hit the wall that was next to the lot.

the boys on walter's tēam picked him up and yelled, "walter kicked for a scōre." the boys from the other tēam said, "you are some football plāyer."

and the boys and girls on the sIde of the lot called, "walter is the star of the gāme." walter was very happy.

and now walter can plāy football with the other boys any tIme he wants.

the end

rēad the Items

1. when the tēacher says "one," hōld up one hand.

2. when the tēacher says "go," stand up.

---

mad	walter	other
māde	wall	another
hōpe	plāyer	there
hop	picked	what
fin	dropped	that
fīne	cannot	want
all	can't	went
almōst	do	were
also	dōn't	where
alwāys	didn't	whȳ

carmen the cow

this is a stōry about a cow nāmed carmen.

when the other cows said "moo," the children alwāys cāme to pet them. but when carmen said "moo," all the children alwāys ran awāy. the children ran awāy bēcause carmen had a loud moo. she trIed to sāy a little moo, but her moo was alwāys a big, loud moo.

the other cows made fun of her. they said, "we do not lIke you bēcause your moo is so loud."

carmen trIed and trIed, but her moo was too loud.

one dāy some children cāme to the farm with a tēacher. they cāme to pet the cows. they petted all the

carmen calls for help

who cāme to the farm to pet cows?

whȳ didn't the children pet carmen?

who fell into a dēēp, dēēp hōle?

how did the other cows trȳ to help the girl?

whȳ didn't the tēacher hēar the cows mooing?

then carmen saw the girl. carmen called "moo" very loud. she called "moo" so loud that the tēacher could hēar her. the tēacher said, "that sounds lIke a call for help." the tēacher ran to the little girl.

the tēacher helped the little girl get out of the hōle. the tēacher went ōver to carmen and said, "we are so glad that you have a loud moo. you said 'moo' so loud that you sāved the little girl."

and what do you think the little girl did? the little girl kissed carmen and said, "thank you for mooing so loud."

now carmen has lots of children pet her. carmen is happy that she has a big, loud moo.

this is the end.

jill's mouse

jill had a pet mouse. her mouse was little and pink. jill got a little box for her little mouse. then she went to her mother and said, "look what I have. I have a pet mouse in this box."

her mother jumped up. her mother said, "get that mouse out of this house."

jill said, "but I want to keep this mouse."

her mother said, "you can't keep that mouse in this house. I don't like that mouse."

jill asked, "would you let me keep this mouse in the yard? then the mouse would not be around you."

"yes," her mother said, "but keep that mouse out of this house."

so Jill took the box and went to the yard. she said, "I will make a house for this mouse." so she piled some grass around the box.

now Jill is happy and her mother is happy. and the mouse is happy.

why was Jill happy?

why was her mother happy?

why was the mouse happy?

the end

1

the magic pouch

there was a little girl who lived
nēar a tall mountain. the mountain
was so tall that the top was alwāys
in the clouds. the girl wanted to
go to the top of the mountain, but
her mother tōld her, "no." she said,
"that mountain is stēēp. you would
fīnd it very hard to get to the top."

but one dāy the little girl was
sitting and looking at the mountain.
she said to herself, "I would līke to
see what is in thōse clouds at the
top of the mountain. I think I
will go up and see."

so the girl took her pet hound
and started up the tall mountain.
they went up and up. the sīde of

the mountain was very stēēp. up
they went. the girl said to her
hound, "do not fall. it is very far
down to the ground."

soon the little girl and her
hound cāme to the clouds nēar the
top of the mountain. she said to her
hound, "now we will see what is on
the other sīde of thōse clouds."

what do you think they will see
on the other sīde of the clouds?

mōre to come

2

the magic pouch

where did the little girl live?

what did the girl want to do?

who tōld her not to go up the
mountain?

who did she tāke with her?

where did the girl go with her
hound?

the little girl and her hound
went into the clouds. she said, "I
cannot see too well. thēse clouds
māke a fog." but the girl and her
hound kept gōiṅg up and up.

all at once they cāme out of the
clouds. they could not see the
ground any mōre. they could ōnly
see clouds under them. they were in
the sun. the sun was in the girl's

eyes, so she could not see well. she sat down and said to her hound, "we must sit and rest."

all at once the little girl looked up and saw a funny little house. she said, "I didn't see that house before. let's go see who lives there."

so the girl and her hound walked over to the funny little house.

all at once a loud sound came from the house.

more to come

3

the magic pouch

where did the little girl and her hound go?

what did they see when they cāme out of the clouds?

what did they hēar coming from the house?

when the loud sound cāme from the house, the little girl stopped. she looked all around, but she did not see anyone. the sound cāme from the house once mōre. the girl and her hound walked up to the house. she called, "is anyone insIde that house?"

all at once the dōōr of the house ōpened. the girl looked insIde the house, but she did not see anyone. slōwly she walked insIde. slōwly her hound walked insIde. then the dōōr slammed bēhInd them. the hound jumped. the girl jumped. she said, "let's get out of hēre." she grabbed the dōōr, but it would not ōpen. the girl said, "I dōn't lIke this."

all at once the girl looked at a funny pouch hanging on the wall. and a loud sound cāme out of the pouch. it said, "ōpen this pouch and let me out."

mōre to come

4

the magic pouch

what did the little girl and her hound see on top of the mountain?

why didn't they leave the funny house?

what was hanging on the wall?

the girl walked over to the pouch. she said, "is there some thing in that pouch?"

"yes. I am a magic elf. I have lived in this pouch for a thousand years. please, would you open the pouch and let me out?"

the little girl asked, "how many years have you lived in that pouch?"

the elf said, "a thousand years."

the girl started to open the pouch. then she stopped. she said, "elf, I dōn't think I should let you out. this is not mȳ house. I should not be hēre."

the elf said, "this is mȳ house. so plēase ōpen the pouch and let me out. if you let me out, I will give you the pouch. it is magic."

the girl touched the pouch. she asked herself, "should I ōpen this pouch and let him out?"

mōre to come

5

the magic pouch

what was insIde the pouch?

how many yēars had the elf lived
in the pouch?

the little girl said to herself,
"should I ōpen this pouch?" she
looked at the pouch. then slōwly she
ōpened it. out jumped a little elf,
no bigger than your foot. the girl's
hound went, "owwwww." then the elf
jumped all around the room. he
jumped on the tāble and on the
flōōr. then he ran up one wall and
down the other wall. he ēven ran
around the hound. "owwwww," the
hound yelled.

"I'm out. I'm out," the elf
shouted. "I lived in that pouch a

thousand yēars and now I'm out."

at last the girl's hound stopped gōīng "owwwww." the elf sat on the tāble and said, "I thank you very much. plēase tāke the magic pouch. but be cāreful. when you are good, the pouch will be good to you. but when you are bad, the pouch will be bad to you.

more to come

6

<u>the magic pouch</u>

the elf tōld the little girl, "when you are bad, the pouch will be bad to you."

the girl picked up the pouch. she said to the elf, "I have been good to you. let's see if this magic pouch will be good to me."

she rēached insIde the pouch and found ten round rocks that shIne. "thēse round rocks are gōld," she shouted. "I'm rich."

so the girl thanked the elf for the pouch.

then the girl and her hound started down the tall mountain. they went down and down. they went into the clouds. when they left the clouds, the girl could see the ground. down and down they went.

when they rēached the bottom of the mountain, the sun was settiñg. it was gettiñg lāte. the girl was tīred. but she ran to her house.

her mother met her at the dōōr. she said, "where were you? your father and I have looked all around for you."

the little girl did not tell her mother where she went. she said, "I went to slēēp in the grass. I just wōke up." she tōld a līe, and that was bad.

mōre to come

7

the magic pouch

did the little girl tell her mother where she was?

what did she tell her mother?

what does the pouch do when you are bad?

the girl's mother looked at the pouch. she said, "where did you get that pouch?"

"I found it on the ground," the little girl said. she tōld another līe. "but mother, there are ten rocks of gōld in this pouch. we are rich."

she rēached in the pouch and took something out. but when she looked, she saw that she was not hōlding gōld rocks. she was hōlding yellōw mud. her mother said, "you are not funny. we are not rich. but you are dirty. go clēan your hands."

the little girl got a rag and trIed to rub the yellōw mud from her hands. but it would not come from her hands. she rubbed and rubbed, but the yellōw mud stāyed on her hands. her mother trIed to get the mud from her hands, but she could not do it.

then the girl started to crȳ.

mōre to come

146

8

the magic pouch

what did the little girl take from the pouch?

could she get the yellōw mud from her hands?

could her mother get the yellōw mud from her hands?

the girl crīed and crīed. then she said, "mother, I tōld you some līes. I did not slēep in the grass. I went to the top of the tall mountain. and I did not fīnd the pouch on the ground. a funny elf gave it to me." the girl tōld her mother all about the funny house and the elf.

and when she looked at her hands, she saw that they were clēan.

her mother said, "where did the mud go?"

"I dōn't see it any where," the girl said. she looked to see if there was more mud inside the pouch. and what do you think was inside the pouch? there were a thousand rocks of gōld. her mother said, "we are rich. we are very rich."

and the little girl said to herself, "that pouch is good to me because I was good. I will kēēp on doiñg good thiñgs." and she did. and every time she was good, she rēached in the pouch and found something good.

no more to come

the bugs and the elephant

five elephants went for a walk. one elephant was very tall. that elephant said, "I must sit and rest. I will look for a spot of ground where I can sit."

so she looked for a good site to sit on the ground. at last she came to a fine site that was in the sun. she said, "this spot is fine." but a flȳ was sitting in that spot. the flȳ said, "go awāy, elephant. this is mȳ spot."

the elephant said, "hō, hō. you cannot stop me if I want to sit in the sun."

so the elephant sat down. that flȳ got out of her wāy. then the elephant said, "this is a fine site. it is fun here."

the flȳ said, "you took mȳ spot.
so I will fix you."

the flȳ went awāy and the
elephant went to slēēp.

when the elephant woke up, she
saw that there were many bugs on
the ground. those bugs were all
around her.

the elephant said, "how did these
bugs get here?"

the little flȳ said, "these bugs are
with me. they are here to take you
awāy."

and they did. they picked up the
elephant and took her to the lake.
then they dropped her in the lake.

now the flȳ is sitting in the sun
and the elephant is sitting in the lake.
the flȳ thinks it is fun to sit in the

sun. and the elephant thinks it is
more fun to sit in the lake.
this is the end.

the pet gōat

a girl got a pet gōat. she liked to go running with her pet gōat. she plāyed with her gōat in her house. she plāyed with the gōat in her yard.

but the gōat did some thiñgs that made the girl's dad mad. the gōat ate thiñgs. he ate cans and he ate canes. he ate pans and he ate panes. he ēven ate capes and caps.

one dāy her dad said, "that gōat must go. he ēats too many thiñgs."

the girl said, "dad, if you let the gōat stāy with us, I will see that he stops ēatiñg all those thiñgs."

her dad said, "we will trȳ it."

so the gōat stāyed and the girl made him stop ēatiñg cans and canes and caps and capes.

but one dāy a car robber came
to the girl's house. he saw a big
red car nēar the house and said, "I
will stēal that car."

he ran to the car and started to
ōpen the dōōr.

the girl and the gōat were plāyiṅg
in the back yard. they did not see
the car robber.

more to come

the goat stops the robber

a girl had a pet goat. her dad had a red car.

a car robber was going to steal her dad's car. the girl and her goat were playing in the back yard.

just then the goat stopped playing. he saw the robber. he bent his head down and started to run for the robber. the robber was bending over the seat of the car. the goat hit him with his sharp horns. the car robber went flying.

the girl's dad ran out of the house. he grabbed the robber. "you were trying to steal my car," he yelled.

the girl said, "but my goat stopped him."

"yes," her dad said. "that gōat saved mȳ car."

the car robber said, "somethinḡ hit me when I was trȳinḡ to stēal that car."

the girl said, "mȳ gōat hit you."

the girl hugged the gōat. her dad said, "that gōat can stāy with us. and he can ēat all the cans and canes and caps and capes he wants."

the girl smiled. her gōat smiled. her dad smiled. but the car robber did not smile. he said, "I am sore."

the end

jane wanted to flȳ, flȳ, flȳ

a girl named jane said, "I want to flȳ, flȳ, flȳ in the skȳ, skȳ, skȳ." her father said, "but if you fall on your head, head, head, you'll end up in bed, bed, bed."

but the girl did not stop talkiñg about flȳiñg. one dāy she went to her dad and said, "if you help me make a big kite, I can flȳ in the skȳ like the birds."

her dad said, "I will help you make a kite, but I dōn't think you should trȳ to flȳ."

jane said, "that is good, good, good. let's make a kite of wood, wood, wood."

her dad said, "we'll nēēd pāper and striñg to make this thiñg."

jane and her dad got pāper and striñg and wood. they made a kite that was very, very big.

jane said, "when the wind starts to blōw, blōw, blōw, just see me go, go, go."

her father said, "no, no, no."

more to come

<u>jane goes up, up, up</u>

a girl named jane wanted to fly,
but her dad didn't want her to fly.
he helped her make a big kite. but he
tōld her that she could not fly with
that kite.

then one dāy, the wind started to
blōw. jane got her big kite. she said,
"I dōn't knōw why, why, why dad
wōn't let me fly, fly, fly."

as she was hōlding the kite, a big
wind started to blōw the kite awāy.
jane said, "I must hōld on to that
kite or it will go far awāy."

so she held on to the kite. but
when the wind started to blōw very
hard, it lifted the kite into the sky.
she looked down and yelled, "I want

my dad, dad, dad, because this is bad, bad, bad."

the kite went up and up. soon it was near the clouds. jane yelled, "now I'm over the town, town, town, but I want to go down, down, down."

at last the kite came down. it landed in a farm five miles from town. jane left the kite there and walked back to her home. then she told her dad, "now I know why, why, why I should not fly, fly, fly."

jane never tried flying again.

the end

the little cloud

there was a little cloud. the little cloud lived in the skȳ with a mother cloud and a father cloud.

the father cloud was very big and very dark. every now and then the father cloud would sāy, "it is time to make some rāin." the father cloud would shake and make loud thunder sounds—"boom, boom." then the rāin would fall from the cloud. the father cloud was very proud. he was the best rāin maker in the skȳ.

but the mother cloud was pretty good at mākiñg rāin too. every now and then she would sāy, "I think I'll make some rāin." she would make some loud thunder sounds, and out would come the rāin.

but the little cloud could not make rāin. he would sāy, "I think I'll make some rāin." he would shake and shake. he would trȳ as hard as he could, but no rāin came from that small cloud.

the mother cloud said, "dōn't fēel bad. when you are bigger, you will make rāin. you are too small now, but you will grōw."

and that small cloud did grōw. every dāy he got a little bigger and a little darker. and every dāy he trĪed to make rāin. but he couldn't ēven make loud sounds. and not one drop of rāin came from that cloud. he felt very sad.

then one dāy something happened. the wind was blōwing very hard.

that wind bēgan to blōw the little cloud far awāy from his mother and father. he called to them. but they werₑ mākiñg loud sounds, so they couldn't hēar him.

more next time

the small cloud must help

the wind was blōwing the small cloud awāy from his father and mother. the small cloud couldn't ēven see them any more. "I am so sad that I will crȳ," the cloud said. but what do you think happened? when the cloud trīed to crȳ, no tēars came out. that made the cloud ēven sadder.

he said, "I am so small that I can't ēven make tēars."

Just then someone called, "help, help."

the little cloud looked down. there was a small dēēr and a mother dēēr. and nēar them was a big forest fire. that small dēēr and the mother dēēr were trapped. "help, help," they called.

the little cloud said to himself, "I must get help." then he called, "mom and dad, come ōver here and make some rāin on the forest." but the mother cloud and the father cloud werₑ too far awāy. they couldn't hēar the little cloud.

"what will I do?" the little cloud asked himself. "if I could make rāin, I could help those dēēr. but I am too small."

the fire was getting bigger all the time. now it was all around the two dēēr. the small cloud said, "I must get mȳ mother and father."

but every time the small cloud started to flōat one wāy, the wind took him back. the small cloud looked down at the two dēēr. then the cloud

said, "I am the ōnly one who can
help those dēēr. so I will do what I
can."

more to come

the small cloud is happy

the little cloud was the ōnly one who could help the two dēēr. the small cloud said, "I will trȳ to rāin. I will trȳ as hard as I can."

the cloud bēgan to shake. he shook and shook and shook. and ēach time he shook, he became a little bigger and a little darker. he shook some more. and he became ēven bigger and darker.

then he bēgan to make loud sounds. "boom, boom," he said. the sounds he made werₑ almōst as loud as his father's sounds. "boom, boom."

and all at once rāin started to fall from the little cloud. two or thrēē drops fell. then more drops bēgan to fall. again the cloud made a loud sound. "boom." the rāin was falliñg faster and faster. it started to fall so fast that it sōaked the forest. it sōaked the trēēs that were on fire. and it sōaked the two dēēr. "thank you, thank you," they called to the cloud. the cloud kept mākiñg rāin. when that cloud stopped, the forest looked like a lake. all of the fires were out, and the dēēr were standiñg in the water.

all at once the mother cloud and the father cloud flōated up to the little cloud. the father cloud said, "we see what you did. you are a good cloud."

the mother cloud said, "I am so proud. todāy mȳ little cloud became a rēal rāin cloud."

this is the end.

the tall m°e, there. I see a

one dāy t'r."

went for a van jumped into the lake.

said, "I ha° all of the bēans and

but I love

the tag said, "I gave the tall

the lake.care, scare, scare. there

the bear ōver there, there, there.

"you c'

arour   the end

grou

said

for

you

like

and

175

sandy counted everything

sandy was a girl who liked to count. she counted things all the time. on her wāy to school, she would count trēēs and dogs and cats. she would count boys and girls. she ēven counted the steps she took.

sandy liked school. the part she liked best was when the tēacher said, "now we will work on counting." sandy was the best counter in the school.

one dāy sandy was walking to school and she was counting things. she was walking nēar the rāil rōad tracks. and a trāin went bȳ. so sandy counted the trāin cars. there were one hundred cars in that trāin.

there were fifty red cars and fifty yellōw cars.

after school was ōver, sandy began to walk home. she walked nēar the rāil rōad tracks. and there was the same trāin she had sēēn before. the trāin was standing on the track. there were two men and one woman in front of the trāin.

one of the men was sāying, "where are the tv sets? they should be on this trāin. but they are missing."

the woman said, "how could they be missing? this trāin has been standing here all dāy. the tv sets were on this trāin before, so they must be on this trāin now."

more to come

sandy fīnds the trāin car

when sandy counted the cars on her wāy to school, there were one hundred cars in the trāin. when she counted the cars after school, there were ninety-nine cars. one car was missing.

sandy said, "I must think about this. there were fifty red cars and fifty yellōw cars. but now there are not fifty red cars. one red car is missing."

sandy walked next to the rāil rōad track.

soon she came to a shed. there were rāil rōad tracks that led to the shed. sandy said to herself, "I will fīnd out what is in that shed."

so sandy follōwed the tracks to
the shed.

she looked inside the shed and
saw a red trāin car standiñg on the
tracks. the car dōōr was ōpen. sandy
looked around. no one was around.
so sandy ran ōver to the dōōr of
the red car and looked inside. the
car was filled with tv sets.

she said to herself, "I found
the car with the tv sets."

sandy was all set to run back to
tell someone that she had found the
missiñg car. but just then there was
a sound nēar her. it was the sound
of foot steps.

more to come

a crook stops sandy

sandy had found the missing train car. but now there was a sound behind her. it was the sound of foot steps.

"I must hide," sandy said.

then she jumped into the red train car and hid behind a big tv set. then she looked out. a big man came into the shed. then another man came in.

one man said, "back your truck up to the end of the shed. we will load the tv sets into the truck. but we must load them fast."

the other man said, "yes." then the men left the shed. sandy said to herself, "these men are crooks. they are stealing the tv sets."

sandy wāited. she could hēar the men talkiñg outside. then she could hēar the sound of the truck.

she said to herself, "I must get out of here." she jumped from the trāin car and began to run as fast as she could go. she ran out of the shed. and then she stopped. the big man was standiñg in front of her.

he said, "what are you doiñg here?"

sandy looked at the man. she wanted to run, but she didn't think that she could run faster than the man. she had to think of somethiñg to sāy. but she couldn't sēēm to talk. she looked at the big man and the big man looked at her.

more to come

sandy tells what she found

sandy trīed to run from the shed but the big man stopped her. he asked her, "what are you doing here?"

sandy wanted to sāy something. but she couldn't think of a thing to sāy.

the big man said, "can't you hēar me? I asked you what you are doing here?"

sandy said, "mȳ hound dog."

"what about your hound dog?" the man asked.

sandy said, "I can't fīnd him. he ran awāy and I was looking for him."

sandy had tōld a big līe. but she

didn't want to tell the big man whȳ she had come to the shed.

the man said, "well, get out of here, and dōn't come back. if I fīnd you plāyiñg around this shed any more, you'll be sorry."

sandy said, "ōkāy. I wōn't come back." she ran awāy from the big man as fast as she could go. she said, "I must tell someone what I found out."

sandy ran back to the trāin that had a car missiñg. the men and the woman werₑ still standiñg nēₐr the trāin. a cop was with them now. sandy ran up to the cop. she yellₑd, "I found the car with the tv sets."

more to come

sandy and big bill

sandy ran up to the cop. she told him that she had found the missing train car.

one man said, "will you get out of here, little girl? can't you see that we are talking?"

sandy said, "but I found the train car that is missing."

the woman said, "there is no missing train car."

sandy said, "but there is a car missing and I found it." then sandy told them all about the missing car.

after she told what had happened, the cop said, "I think there were one hundred cars in that train. how can we check it?"

one man said, "that's ēasy. I'll get big bill. he counts the cars on every trāin that comes in here."

that man left. soon he came back with another man. as he walked back with the other man he shouted, "big bill counted the cars. he says that there are ninety-nine cars."

sandy looked at big bill, and big bill looked at sandy. big bill was the man who had stopped her outside the shed.

more to come

back to the shed

sandy saw that big bill was the big man who had stopped her outside the shed. she shouted, "that's one of the men who was stēaling the tv sets. that's him." she tōld the cop that big bill had stopped her outside the shed.

big bill looked very mēan. he said, "what's that girl talkĩng about? I think she's nuts."

sandy said, "no, I'm not nuts. that is one of the men."

big bill said, "I dōn't knōw what she is talkĩng about. I never saw her before. and I dōn't knōw anythĩng about a shed with a red trāin car in it."

"yes, you do," sandy said.

the cop said, "well, why dōn't we all take a walk down the tracks and fīnd out who is lȳiñg?"

so they all walkᵉd down the tracks to the shed. when they came nēₐr the shed, sandy could see a big white truck at one end of the shed. she said, "that must be their truck. the crooks must be inside the shed, lōₐdiñg the truck."

big bill gave sandy a mēₐn look.

more to come

thank you, sandy

sandy and the others wer_e nēar the shed. the cop said, "the rest of you wāit here. I'll go inside that shed and see what's gōing on."

so they wāited as the cop went into the shed. as soon as the cop was in the shed, big bill said, "I've got work to do. I'm lēaving."

"you better stāy here," one of the men said. big bill didn't answer. bill just gave sandy a mēan look.

sandy looked at the shed and wāited. then she saw some men start to come from the shed. they all had their hands up. the cop was walking behind them.

the cop shouted, "that girl found the tv sets. I think big bill is one of the crooks."

one of the men said to sandy, "thank you for fInding the missing car." the woman also thanked sandy. so did the cop.

then one of the men said, "this rāil rōad would like to give you a gift for fInding the crooks." so the man gave her a very fine gift. what do you think that gift was?

it was a tv set.

this is the end.

sam gets a kite kit

sam liked to make things. he
liked to make toy cars. so he went
to the store and got a toy car kit.
his mom said, "that kit has the parts
of a car. you have to rēad and fīnd
out how to fit the parts so that they
make a car."

sam said, "I will do that."

so sam began to rēad the pāper
that came with the car kit. then he
began to fit the parts to make a car.
soon he had a toy car.

his mom said, "that is a fine car.
you are good at rēading and at
making things."

sam did not like to make the
same thing again. he said, "I will

not make other cars. I will make
something else."

so he went to the store and got
a kite kit. when he got home, he
shōwed his mom the kite kit. his mom
said, "that kit has a lot of parts in
it. you will have to rēad the pāper
that comes with the kit to fīnd
out how to make the kite."

sam looked inside the kit. then he
said, "what pāper? there is no pāper
in this kit."

sam's mom said, "that is too bad.
how will you make the kite if there
is no pāper in the kit?"

sam said, "I will go back to the
store and get a pāper that tells how
to make a kite from these parts."

when sam got to the store, the man in the store said, "I dōn't have other pāpers that tell how to make kites."

sam asked, "how can I make a kite if I dōn't have the pāper?"

the man said, "you will have to do the best you can."

sam was not happy. he went home and looked at all the parts in the kite kit.

more to come

sam makes a funny kite

sam liked to make things. he had made a toy car from a kit. he did a good job. now sam had a kite kit. but there was no pāper in the kit to tell how to make a kite from the parts.

sam was not very happy. he looked at ēach of the parts. then he began to trȳ to make a kite from the parts in the kit. he worked and worked.

when his mom saw the kite, she said, "hō, hō. that is a funny-looking kite."

it was funny-looking. it looked like a small tent made out of pāper and wood. the top of the kite was very sharp.

sam's mom said, "I'm sorry for making fun of your kite, but it looks very funny."

sam said, "I dōn't care how funny it looks. I think it will flȳ."

his mom said, "no, I dōn't think it will. it does not look like a kite that will flȳ."

"we will see," sam said.

so sam and his mom went to the park. there were lots of boys and girls in the park. some of them were flȳing kites. and some of the kites were wāy up in the skȳ.

sam said, "I think mȳ kite will pass up all those kites."

sam's mom said, "I dōn't think your kite will go thrēē fēēt from the ground."

do you think sam's kite will flȳ?
more next time

can sam's kite rēally flȳ?

when sam made his kite, his mom said that it looked funny. so did the boys and girls in the park. they looked at the kite and said, "hō, hō, that thing looks like a tent. it wōn't flȳ."

sam said, "we will see."

sam's kite began to go up. up, up it went. it was going up very fast. sam's mom said, "well, would you look at that kite go up."

the boys and girls said, "wow, that kite can rēally flȳ."

soon sam's kite passed up all the other kites. it went up so far it looked like a little spot.

some of the boys and girls asked sam, "where did you get that kite?"

sam said, "you can get a kit for

this kite at the toy store. but I will have to tell you how to fit the parts so that they make a tent kite."

more and more boys and girls asked sam about his kite. at last sam said, "I will make a pāper that tells how to make a tent kite from the kit."

and he did. when he got home, he sat down with his mom. his mom helped him with the pāper. when they were done, his mom said, "this pāper rēads very well. you did a good job."

sam said, "that's good. now let's make a lot of these pāpers so we can give one to everybody who wants one."

the next dāy sam gave ēach boy and girl a pāper. he tōld them to rēad the pāper and do what it said.

now there are many tent kites

flȳing ōver the park. and no one
says, "hō, hō." the tent kites flȳ
better than any other kite.
the end

tim and his hat

tim had a hat. it was red and white. tim said, "I hate this hat." but his mother said, "it is cōld outside. so you must have a hat."

when tim was outside, he said, "I will take this hat and hide it." so he did. he found an ōld trēē with a hole in it. he stuck the hat in the hole. then he said, "when I come back from school, I will get mȳ hat from the trēē."

tim got to school on time. he began rēading his book. then he looked out the windōw. what do you think was falling from the skȳ? snōw was falling. when tim saw the snōw, he said, "wow, it is getting cōld out there." and it was. it was getting cōlder and cōlder.

when school was ōver, the snōw
was very dēēp. tim walked outside.
then he said, "mȳ ēars are getting
cōld. I had better run home." so
tim began to run. he ran as fast as
he could go, but the snōw was very
dēēp and it was hard to run in that
snōw. the other boys and girls were
plāying in the snōw, but tim did not
have time to plāy. he said, "I must
get home before mȳ ēars get too
cōld."

at last, tim came to the ōld trēē.
he grabbed his red and white hat.
he slipped the hat ōver his ēars.
then he said, "I dōn't hate this hat.
I like this hat now."

tim did not hate his hat after

that dāy. and he did not hide his hat
in trēēs. now tim has time to plāy
with the other boys and girls when
the snōw gets dēēp.

this stōry is ōver.

212

the fox wants a cone

a little girl was sitting in the
woods. she had an ice crēam cone.
she was sitting on a log, ēating her
ice crēam cone.

a slȳ fox was looking at her. that
fox was thinking. "I will con that
girl. I will con her into giving me
her cone."

so the slȳ fox ran up to the girl.
then he fell ōver and began to
shout, "help me, help me. mȳ
mouth is on fire. give me something
cool for mȳ mouth."

"close your eyes and ōpen your
mouth," the girl said.

the slȳ fox was thinking, "hō, hō,
I conned that girl out of her cone."

when the fox closed his eyes, he

did not get a cone in his mouth. he
got a drink of cōld water.

"there," the girl said. "that
should make your mouth cool."

"no, no," the fox shouted. "mȳ
mouth nēēds something cōlder than
that water."

the girl said, "close your eyes
and ōpen your mouth."

the fox said to himself, "this
time I will con her out of her
cone."

but he did not con her out of a
cone. he conned her out of a bit of
ice. she dropped the ice into his
mouth. then she said, "now your
mouth must fēēl cool."

"no, no," the fox yelled. "I nēēd
a cone."

the girl said, "you can have the cone, but I ate all the ice crēam."

but the fox did not take the cone. she had made him so mad that he ran back into the woods. he never trIed to con her again.

more to come

<u>rēad the Item</u>

sāy "what" when the tēacher says "that."

<u>the con fox</u>

the slȳ fox wanted an ice crēam cone. he couldn't con the girl out of her cone, but he had a plan. he said, "I will go to the ice crēam stand. when I get there, I will con somebody out of a cone."

so that fox went to town. when he came to the ice crēam stand, he said, "hand me a cone."

the man at the stand made up a big cone. then the man said, "that will be one dime."

the fox said, "but I gave you a dime."

the man said, "no, you did not give me a dime. I think you are trȳing to con me."

"I dōn't con men," the fox said. "I

came here for a cone. and I gave you a
dime for that cone."

the man looked at that sly fox. then
the man said, "if this is not a trick, I will
give you the cone."

the fox said, "I am not lying. I am
not trying to con you."

just then a little girl came up to the
ice cream stand. it was the girl that the
fox had met in the woods. the girl said to
the fox, "you are the fox that tried to
con me out of my cone. I am glad to
see that you are buying a cone."

the man at the stand said, "so you
are a con fox."

the fox was so mad that he ran back
to the woods. he never tried to con the
man at the cone stand again.

this is the end.

rēad the Item

say "spot" if the tēacher says "stop."

don was sad

don had a job that he did not like. he worked in a hat store. he mopped up in that store at the end of ēach dāy. every dāy he mopped and mopped. when he mopped, he talked to himself. he would sāy, "I hate to work in this hat store. I hate to mop."

then he would think of things that he would like to do. he said, "I wish I was big. I wish I could flȳ. I would like to be a super man. but I am just a mopper. I am not big. I cannot flȳ."

when the store was mopped, don would sit and mope. he would think of the things he would do if he was a super man.

"I would fīnd crooks," he said. "they would shoot at me, but I would not fēēl a thing."

every dāy was the same. don would mop and mop. then he would mope and mope. when he mopped, he would think about being a super man. when he would mope, he would think about that too.

then one dāy something happened. don was mopping in the back of the store. all at once, he stopped mopping. "I think I hēar something," he said.

the sound came from the dōōr that led down the stāirs. somebody was sāying, "come down the stāirs." don ōpened the dōōr and went down the stāirs.

to be continued

r̄ead the Item

when the t̄eacher says "what," s̄ay "that."

don mēēts a woman

wher_e did don work?

wh̄y did don mope?

somebody t̄old don to come down the stāirs. so don dropp_ed his mop and went down the stāirs. it was very dim down ther_e. but don could see a woman in the dark. the woman had a cap and a cape. she said, "don, do you want to be a super man?"

"yes, I do," don said.

the woman said, "I will help you be a super man if you tell me that you will do good."

"I will do good," don said.

then the woman handed don a dime. that dime look_ed dim in the dark.

the woman said, "kēēp that dime. when you want to be a super man, tap the dime thrēē times."

don looked at the dime, but when he looked up, he did not see the woman. "where are you?" don asked.

there was no answer. don called again, but there was no answer. then don took the dime and went up the dim stāirs. he said to himself, "I must be having a drēam." but then he looked at the dime and said, "if I am drēaming, how did I get this dime?"

don picked up his mop and began to mop again. then he said, "I think I will tap that dime thrēē times and see what happens. I hope it works."

so don dropped his mop and tapped his dime one time, two times, thrēē times.

to be continued